BASIC WRITING SKILLS

by Carlin Kindilien, Ph.D.

ARCO PUBLISHING, INC.
NEW YORK

Published by Arco Publishing, Inc.
219 Park Avenue South, New York, N.Y. 10003

Library of Congress Cataloging in Publication Data
Kindilien, Carlin T.

  Basic writing skills.
  1. English language—Rhetoric.   I. Title.
PE1408.K646   808'.042   81-10819

ISBN 0-668-05264-3   AACR2

Printed in the United States of America

Contents

STAGE #4—REVISING
Good writing is revised writing

SOME FAMILIAR WRITING FORMS
Business letters, persuasive articles, and term papers

PART FIVE   ONE MORE TIME

ONE MORE TIME
Writing skills are the result of a mastery of the
following elements and techniques: specific subjects
and action verbs; short, simple sentences; paragraphs
as the writing unit; transitional words and phrases;
and exhaustive revision

PART SIX   A GUIDE TO GRAMMAR AND PUNCTUATION

A GUIDE TO GRAMMAR AND PUNCTUATION

Preface

Who am I to tell you about writing? And what do I want to tell you?

I am someone who has developed a few convictions about writing. These are reinforced daily by my pleasure in reading and writing—and by the happy fact that writing has long paid our family's bills.

First, the pleasures. While it may not challenge a scrumptious meal or a loving relationship, writing is a joy. Yes, it is hard work, disciplined work. But many years ago my high school English teacher, Miss Ruth McMahon, told us that one of the true pleasures in life is to see something that impresses and be able to describe it in words. With every new year, I mark how right she was. I want to share that pleasure with my children, my friends, and anyone else who cares to read.

Some of you may read on because I make my living as a writer. Certainly, writing has been the common denominator of my life. I have spent my working life as student, marine, linesman, hodcarrier, teacher, technical writer, editor, supervisor, manager, dean, professor, administrator, department head, and director. During the off-hours I played football and hockey, I fished every chance I had, and there were gardens and camps and some long hikes. In all of these activities, whether for livelihood or fun, writing has been the touchstone. Book reports, letters to the editor, theses, business letters, travel articles, fishing stories, dissertations, reports, specifications, briefs, resumes, short stories, novels, poems, technical manuals, books, pamphlets, guidebooks, how-to books, and, always, letters and notes for more writing. I cannot imagine a life without writing.

That is who I am. And what do I want to tell you about writing? I especially want to shout that writing is not as difficult a chore as you have been led to, or have let yourself, believe. While it is not as easy as talking, it is part of the same natural process. Relying on your instinct for language and your common sense, I can quickly show you how to write a sentence and how to put a few of them together in a chronologically ordered paragraph. You can handle many of your writing chores with nothing more than that. In a very few pages, in a very few exercises, you can master the basic writing skills. After that, your discipline and your genius will see you through the writing of a business letter or a historical novel, a diary entry or a five-year plan for your company, a final examination or a poem.

This book is short. Another of my convictions is that students of writing should *write*. In this book I have tried to keep my words about the writing guidelines as few as possible. The core of the book is the writing exercises. Teachers and students, I believe, should interface with a piece of writing. It is at this point that the student needs help, needs answers, needs direction. That is why when I teach a course in writing I ask that all of the writing be done in class, where the student and I can confront the writing problem together.

Since we cannot meet in class, this book is my offering to those who want to improve their writing skills. I have included all of the advice I think necessary to get started. The conventional grammar and composition books with their full discussions are easily come by for those who want more information. The frequent exercises in my book build toward a mastery of the essentials. The exercises are not the kind that demand close correction. You will know well enough if you have mastered and demonstrated the principle. But if you want another's opinion—particularly with the final exercise—seek out a teacher, a colleague, or a friend—anyone who can judge your writing.

The words in this book are mine; the ideas are distilled from many teachers, many books, and many editors. The influence of those who shape our convictions never stops. I began to write under the wary eyes of the Sisters of Mercy. They fashioned the loops and swirls that became my words, and they revealed the intricate beauty of the English sentence in chalky diagrams. Ruth McMahon simply loved to teach English; I learned from her how to run with words. My freshman English teacher at St. Bonaventure was Thomas Merton. He was not much of a classroom teacher. (We copied dictionary entries while he contemplated his withdrawal. He left us in the spring. We felt responsible.) But his textbook forcefully urged UNITY, COHERENCE, EMPHASIS, and INTEREST as the fundamental writing principles. Not bad advice. There was Professor William T. Hastings, a Shakespearean scholar at Brown University, who tore one of my first graduate school papers apart and sent me back to the composition books. More recently, Jim Fox and Mark Hanover and Rene Bernier and Leon Hull, friends and editors, and many others until Ruth Billard wrote a dozen pages of commentary on an early draft of this book. I cannot remember or dig out the name of the person who suggested the four-stage writing procedure. I suspect it came from a text on report writing back in the early sixties. My contribution to that idea is to extend it to all writing forms.

The thinking, the planning, the writing, the revising: these are the keys to the basic writing skills. To all who shared them with me, my thanks.

Carlin Kindilien

FIRST THINGS

First Things...

Get Into the Right Frame of Mind for Writing

So you are afraid to write. You tried long ago or last night, and nothing much came of the effort. The blank sheet grew blanker as you stared at it.

Take heart. You have more going for you than you might imagine. What, exactly?

- **WRITING IS A NATURAL PROCESS**—as natural as eating, swimming, talking. No one had to teach you to speak. Yet by age three or four you had a vocabulary of 1000 words—and you were making sentences. Your own sentences.

- **YOU HAVE BEEN COMMUNICATING WITH OTHER PEOPLE MOST OF YOUR LIFE.** Long before you appeared in kindergarten, you were able to sort out your

3

words to plead, scold, purr, swear, and cheer. When you learned to talk you mastered a complex language.

- **YOU HAVE AN INSTINCT FOR LANGUAGE**—a sense of what is right or wrong. You know what works and what does not when you resort to words. Nine times out of ten what sounds right to you will turn out to be correct grammar.

- **YOUR VOCABULARY WILL TAKE CARE OF IT-SELF.** You need neither big words nor many of them to get your ideas across to a reader simply and clearly. Right now, you probably have all the words you will ever need for your writing. A child with a 12-word vocabulary could, mathematicians tell us, compose over 400 million different "sentences." That is plenty.

WHAT IS AHEAD?

In the following pages, you will review some fundamental matters of language and writing. First, you will learn how to build a sentence around subjects and verbs and then how to arrange these sentences in a readable paragraph. Once you have grasped what a sentence is all about and have seen how to line up your ideas on a page, the rest is practice. WRITING PRACTICE.

Here in a single sentence is this book's main idea. This is what you will learn:

THE BASIC WRITING SKILLS RESULT FROM A MASTERY OF THESE ELEMENTS AND TECHNIQUES: SPECIFIC SUBJECTS AND ACTION VERBS; SHORT, SIMPLE SENTENCES; PARAGRAPHS AS THE WRITING UNIT; TRANSITIONAL WORDS AND PHRASES; AND EXHAUSTIVE REVISION.

HOW LONG WILL IT TAKE?

That depends on your previous exposure to the writing experience, on the extent of your reading to date, and *especially* on the concentration and effort you are prepared to expend.

We are talking hours and days, not months and years. Anyone who speaks and reads English can learn to use the basic writing skills in a single day.

What that person does with these skills is another matter—a matter of discipline, incentive, genius.

WHAT SPECIAL QUALIFICATIONS DO I NEED FOR THIS APPROACH?

Only an ability to speak and read the English language.

We do count on your language sense—and your common sense.

And we take for granted your incentive to write. The fact of your reading this far indicates that you have discovered that you must write in the course of your daily activities. And be judged, in part, on that writing.

Why do we write? To give directions, to explain, to persuade, to report what happened, to summarize another person's ideas: these are some of the important reasons. They are reason enough for most of us to learn the basic writing skills.

Here Are the Essentials... All You Need to Understand About Writing to Get Started... in the Briefest of Reviews

> **Your goal as a writer is to express yourself simply and clearly so that your meaning can be easily grasped by a reader.**

One way to make it easy going for our readers is to do some <u>hard</u> writing. Not the laborious "hard." Rather, a hard concentration on the basic guidelines.

Guideline #1: Specific Subjects and Action Verbs

- A **SUBJECT** names someone or something. It identifies a doer. Note the underlined subjects in these examples:

The new president promised action.

Weathermen predicted rain.

The canoe capsized.

The fire siren screamed.

The dog snarled.

- A **VERB** tells something about a subject. It makes a statement about the doer. Consider the action of the verbs underlined by a wavy line.

The skaters whirled by.

The coffee spilled on the rug.

The bride tossed the flowers.

Sixty people die each day in traffic accidents.

The frozen pipe burst.

• Subjects and verbs are the backbone of every paragraph. Together, they make sense. They combine to form a complete (in their context) and independent statement. If they are fuzzy and general, rather than clear and specific, the paragraph will fall apart.

> **EVERY SENTENCE YOU WRITE IS A PROBLEM OF SUBJECT AND VERB RELATIONSHIP.**

Guideline #2: Short, Simple Sentences

• A simple sentence is the basic sentence pattern of the English language. In its essential form, the simple sentence contains a verb that makes a complete statement about its subject. That is all.

The Senate adjourned yesterday.

The goalie flung himself toward the ball.

The black cat stalked the alley.

The crowd applauded wildly.

The halfback rolled to his right.

- Note how few words it takes to make a clear, complete statement. The short sentence is a hallmark of clear writing.

- Another way to ensure that your reader understands what you write is to limit each of your sentences to a single idea or to a couple of closely related ones. Break your thought into small blocks of meaning.

You're looking for your first job. You're eighteen or twenty-two, and the free ride is almost over. The schooling, the paper route, the chores, the summer jobs are behind you. You want a real job—full-time, permanent.

> **DO NOT UNDERESTIMATE THE SIMPLE SENTENCE. IN MANY WRITING SITUATIONS, IT WILL DO THE WHOLE JOB FOR YOU.**

Guideline #3: Paragraphs As the Writing Unit

- Paragraphs come in all shapes and sizes, and they serve many purposes. The conventional definition is that a paragraph is a collection of sentences dealing with a single idea.

- You will find it more helpful to think of paragraphing as punctuation. The indentation and the white space around a paragraph signal the reader that this is a block of the writer's thought, a unit in the presentation.

- When he paragraphs, a writer breaks his thought into units that are readily grasped by his reader. Paragraphing is a means of leading the reader along in easy stages. Imagine a newspaper page without paragraphs. Slow reading.

- In writing sentences, you start with a subject and verb and then refine or focus your statement with modifiers. In writing paragraphs, you start with a subject (an idea/a topic) and you refine or focus your statement with sentences. The process of defining and describing an idea is the same.

- Organizing sentences within a paragraph is not difficult. Here are two easy-to-use methods of arranging sentences in a paragraph:

  (1) Set down your sentences in chronological order. Use the actual time frame to tell what happened first, second, third. Nothing could be easier to write—or to read.

    Three major sporting events have been scheduled this week for the Civic Auditorium. Today, the final game of the National Invitational Basketball series takes place with Notre Dame opposing Stanford. Tomorrow, professional hockey returns with a playoff position at stake as Minnesota confronts Montreal. On Wednesday, the National Gymnastic Association will sponsor a joint United States-Rumania program, featuring the major Olympic contestants from each country.

  (2) Since most paragraphs are built around some combination of general statements and specific detail, a writer has two obvious choices: either to begin with a

general statement and then supply the necessary supporting detail, or to start with the detail and lead up to a generalization. The choice depends on the difficulty of the subject matter (does the general statement need to be prepared for?) and the emphasis desired (the end of the paragraph is the most emphatic position).

GENERALIZATION ⟶ DETAIL

The rising prime rate is a source of great concern to small companies. Since the prime rate is only offered to a bank's largest customers, the small businesses know they will have to pay much more than the prime rate for their money. Moreover, the smaller companies don't have the other sources of credit that are open to the biggest borrowers.

DETAIL ⟶ GENERALIZATION

The woodpecker drills into the bark of trees with its chisel-like bill and darts a long tongue after the beetles burrowing deep under the bark. The brown creeper moves along the tree trunk dissecting insects away from the recesses of the bark with its delicately decurved bill, while the nuthatch marches headfirst down the tree trunk, seeing things the upright birds have missed. All these birds use the same tree trunk, but each uses it in a special way. (from Ruth Sawyer Billard's Birdscaping Your Yard)

Guideline #4: Transitional Words and Phrases

- Transitional words, phrases, and devices are the nuts and bolts of paragraph writing. They are the writer's chief means of tying sentences together, of making connections and relationships clear, and of speeding a reader's understanding of what is going on within a paragraph.

- There are three useful ways of ensuring a reader's comfortable transition through a paragraph:

   (1) repeating a key word or phrase used in an earlier sentence

   (2) using a pronoun to refer to a word in a preceding sentence

   (3) using transitional expressions like *but, first, on the other hand, also, therefore, finally, in other words, at the same time*, etc.

- Note how transitions are used to guide a reader in this excerpt:

   The WRITING SKILLS WORKSHOP starts with the premise that writing is a natural process. Initially, <u>it</u> builds on the human instinct for language, our sense of right and wrong, of what works and what doesn't work in <u>writing</u>.

By means of unique exercises, participants concentrate on the subject and the verb of their writing—the thing and the doing. Quickly, they learn to arrange them in simple sentences, then in a variety of sentence patterns, each appropriate for a specific thought process. Once they have mastered sentence structure, they are shown how to line up their ideas on a page in highly readable paragraphs. Finally, and most importantly, each member of this WORKSHOP gains new insight into the most neglected phase of the writing process: revision. Each participant leaves the WORKSHOP not with the promise of some day writing but with a finished piece of writing in hand.

Guideline #5: Exhaustive Revision

Now we come onto soggy ground. This guideline on revision is difficult to demonstrate in a short space. There are exceptions, moreover, that permit the inexperienced to escape. Nevertheless . . .

● Effective writing is nearly always revised writing. Granted, some good, even great, writing emerges in first drafts. Yet most of us write first drafts that are too long, too inexact in their word choice, too vague in their detail, too fuzzy in their thought. MOST OF US MUST REVISE—ONCE, TWICE, TEN TIMES.

> **REVISION IS AN INESCAPABLE AND INDISPENSABLE PART OF THE WRITING PROCESS.**

- The key to a successful revision lies not in rules (we will provide many, however) but in attitude. Whenever you write, make the critical assumption that you are writing a first draft and <u>that</u> <u>there</u> <u>will</u> <u>be</u> <u>a</u> <u>second</u> <u>one</u>. That is half the revision battle.

- Revision involves two considerations: (1) the content and clarity of your writing, and (2) its correctness and appropriateness.

A Writing Procedure

All of the guidelines meld into a writing procedure. In any piece of effective writing, whether it be a short business letter or a long technical report, a writer should pass through four stages. The time spent in each of these stages will vary with the complexity of the writing problem, but none can be ignored.

1. **THINK.** In this first stage of preliminary thinking, the writer examines the possibilities and the limitations of an idea. The most critical question: IS THE IDEA WORTH WRITING ABOUT? If it is, the writer should be able to phrase a single sentence that summarizes his idea.

2. **PLAN.** We would all rather write than plan. Writing is easier than thinking. But planning is the only way to be sure that when you start writing, you know where you are

going and where you are stopping. It is the only way to be certain that a reader will accept an idea or an argument. Use an outline or any logical method of organizing that works.

3. **WRITE.** The job here is to flesh out the plan, to get a line of thought down on paper. In this first and roughest of drafts the writer's concern is to catch a flow of thought, to get the story told, to reach an end. The precise phrasing and the correct grammar will come later.

4. **REVISE.** In this final stage—which lasts as long as the writer's stamina—the writer confronts the first draft. Depending on what she reads in her best critical mood, she will condense, expand, or start over. This stage focuses on the writing's content and clarity, on its correctness and appropriateness.

SENTENCES

Basic Sentence Patterns

At this point we begin a more detailed review of the writing guidelines. First, and most important, we will review the three basic sentence patterns.

> NOTE: The final section of this book is a brief guide to grammar, punctuation, and some other formalities of the English language. Most of our detailed discussions of rules and regulations will be left for that section. You can refer to it now, later, anytime.

Basic Sentence Pattern #1

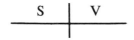

We see, we think, we feel. These observations, these ideas, these sensations consciously register in our brain as words. When we want to communicate an observation, an idea, or a sensation to someone else, we mentally arrange words in patterns called sentences.

A SENTENCE IS A GROUP OF WORDS WITH A SUBJECT AND A VERB THAT TOGETHER MAKE A COMPLETE STATEMENT.

A STATEMENT IS SIMPLY A SUBJECT THAT IS DOING SOMETHING.

Subject	Verb
Taxi	*stopped.*
Lights	*flickered.*
Flowers	*blossomed.*

The SUBJECT names someone or something. It identifies a doer.	**The VERB tells something about the doer. It makes a statement about the doer.**

Together, a subject and a verb make a statement. If that statement makes sense, and if it is a complete statement in its context, then we have a sentence.

WRITE • WRITE • WRITE • WRITE • WRITE • WRITE

Fill a page with your own two-word sentences. Think subject, verb, completeness. For raw material, look around the room (*Door opens. Curtains billow. Papers rustle. Pen falls.*); think of your favorite sport (*Houston rallied. Patriots faded. Ball rolled. Coach fainted.*); or find examples in your work (*Telephone rang. Coffee-break ended. Friday arrived.*) Put a straight line under each subject and a wavy line under each verb.

Length has no bearing on whether a group of words is or is not a sentence. Complete sentences can contain 100 words or one word.

Once you have completed this exercise, you will have mastered the basic sentence pattern: a sentence with a verb that by itself makes a complete statement about its subject. Now you take this simple pattern, add to it, modify it, expand it. It is the building block of effective writing.

MORE ON SPECIFIC SUBJECTS AND ACTION VERBS

- If you want to say something clearly, you must identify the "thing" you are talking about and describe what it is doing. The identification of the thing is easier than the description of the action. That is why the strength of a sentence lies in the verb's action.

- **SUBJECT:** This is the thing you are talking about in the sentence. It is the doer, the sentence workhorse. The more specific your subject, the easier will be your reader's understanding of what you are talking about. If you write *furniture*, the reader has a general idea of your subject. If you write *chair* or *workbench*, that reader has a much clearer idea, because she can see the object in her mind's eye. She sees a *desk*; she does not see *furniture*.

- **VERB:** This is the action word of the sentence. It tells as forcefully as possible what the subject is doing. A verb can express many conditions, but basically, it is a mover. It moves your subject where you want it to go.

- Your goal is an action verb that helps you make a point. Instead of *Diesel engines are in more American cars,* prefer *Diesel engines power many American cars.* Specific verbs like *power* tell a reader more than *are* tells. Strive for action. Stay away from dull verbs like *use* and *utilize.* The carpenter does not *use* a hammer to drive the nail; he *hammers* the nail.

• Most English words come from two sources: Latin and Anglo-Saxon. You do not have to be a scholar to spot the difference. Latin root words (*domicile, nutriment*) are often long and cumbersome. Anglo-Saxon root words (*house, food*) are typically short and familiar. There is nothing wrong with using a Latin root word when it does the job, but Anglo-Saxon root words should be your norm.

REMEMBER

SUBJECTS: The more specific, the better. Identify as exactly as possible the person or thing you will be talking about. Give the reader a picture he can relate to.

VERBS: This action word tells as vividly as possible what the subject is doing. When a verb moves as it should, it is a powerhouse. It *runs, jumps, destroys, paralyzes, sweats, steams*, and *flames*. It *murders, topples*, and *gushes*. It *slaps, smashes*, and *hurtles*.

WRITE • WRITE • WRITE • WRITE • WRITE • WRITE

Go back to the last exercise (two-word sentences) and make your original subjects more specific, your verbs more lively. For example,

INSTEAD OF	A BETTER CHOICE
The plane landed.	*The 747 lumbered in.*
The students protested.	*Fifty freshmen balked.*
Prices increased.	*Grocery costs skyrocketed.*

Again, after you have made your revisions, put a straight line under each subject and a wavy one under each verb.

Basic Sentence Pattern #2

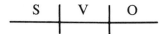

- In the second basic sentence pattern another kind of word comes after the subject and verb and completes the meaning.

Subject	Verb	Object
She	*presented*	*her passport.*
The young man	*wanted*	*a car loan.*
The halfback	*made*	*a quick move.*

Words like *passport, loan,* and *move* are called objects or complements. They complete a meaning left open by the verb. In the examples above, the subjects and verbs alone do not make complete statements.

- **ACTIVE VERSUS PASSIVE SENTENCES:** Both of the sentence patterns we have looked at thus far make statements in which the subject itself is doing something, is acting. This is called an active (as opposed to a passive) sentence because the subject acts (*Jerry coached the tennis team.*). In a passive sentence, the subject receives the action (*The tennis team was coached by Jerry.*). In your writing, use the active voice whenever possible. It is more direct, less wordy than the passive. Occasionally, the passive is useful. If you do not know who or what acts, you will have to use it (*Five new automobiles were stolen.*).

WRITE • WRITE • WRITE • WRITE • WRITE • WRITE

Fill the space below with your own examples of the second basic sentence pattern: the three-part structure of subject, verb, object. Use only active verbs. In this pattern, the action starts with the subject and ends with an object. Use as specific words as possible. For example,

> *The architects drew new plans.*
>
> *Jack birdied the hole.*
>
> *The supertanker absorbed the impact.*
>
> *The doctor dropped the chart.*
>
> *The supervisor signed the timecard.*

Finally, underline the subject (straight lines) and verbs (wavy lines).

Basic Sentence Pattern #3

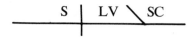

- There is only one other type of statement that can be made with an English sentence. That is a statement in which one asserts that the subject is equal to something else. This sentence pattern is identified by its **LINKING VERB.**

- A linking verb does not express action. It expresses a state of being (*is, appears*) and connects a subject with the word that completes its meaning—a **SUBJECT COMPLEMENT.** This complement can be a noun (*My brother is an accountant.*) or an adjective (*My brother sounds angry.*).

Subject	Linking Verb	Subject Complement

Note that this line points back to the subject.

John Cook	*is*	*the office manager.*
The time	*is*	*short.*
The music	*sounds*	*lively.*
The jacket	*seems*	*tight.*

- Some of the most common linking verbs are *be, became, grow, seem, look, sound, smell, taste,* and *feel.* You will have to recognize linking verbs because they must be followed by adjectives rather than adverbs, which follow action verbs.

    He appeared nervous. (Adjective after linking verb.)

    He paced nervously. (Adverb after action verb.)

> **REMEMBER: a linking verb does not show action. It merely connects a subject and the word that completes its meaning. Subjects and linking verbs alone cannot make a complete statement.**

WRITE • WRITE • WRITE • WRITE • WRITE • WRITE

Begin by writing a dozen examples of the third basic sentence pattern: subject, linking verb, subject complement (predicate noun or adjective). Use some form of the verb *be* as the linking verb (*is, am, are, was, were*). For example: *He is the class secretary. I am free. They are soldiers. Murphy was the editor.*

Now fill the rest of the page with sentences that use a form of a linking verb like *seem, become, appear, look, feel,* and *get* (when it means *become*). For example: *I became the president. I feel sick. You look great. He appears weak. I get tired.*

Again, when you are finished, underline every subject (straight line) and every linking verb (wavy line).

Expanding the Basic Patterns

- Usually, when we write a sentence, we not only name the thing and tell what it is doing but also provide other information about the thing and the doing. We comment. We modify.

MODIFICATION

- Think of MODIFICATION—adjectives, adverbs, phrases, and verbals—as a kind of commentary on the idea you are trying to define for your readers. Some of the most useful modifiers are described below.

- **ADJECTIVE:** This is a describing or limiting word which usually comes before the noun it modifies.

    The jogger held a <u>steady</u> pace.

    <u>This</u> account is overdue.

    He filed <u>several</u> folders.

30

- **ADVERB:** Another describing word, an adverb describes verbs, adjectives, or other adverbs. Adverbs are very democratic. They appear as modifiers almost anywhere in a sentence. Consequently, you will not be able to spot an adverb by its position in the sentence. Adverbs, however, are readily identified by their functions. They are used to answer the following questions: when (*now, today*), how (*quickly, slowly*), where (*there, upstairs*), and to what extent (*very, highly*). Most adverbs are formed by adding -ly to adjectives (*rapid, rapidly*). A few adverbs have the same form as adjectives (*fast*).

Her new job starts today.

I left the keys upstairs.

His pulse rate rose slowly.

The movie was highly recommended.

The TV audience fell off rapidly.

WRITE • WRITE • WRITE • WRITE • WRITE • WRITE

You are now learning to expand the basic sentence structure by modification. Go back to the first writing exercise (two-word sentences) and use your examples as the starting point for this new exercise. Rewrite those sentences and put an adjective in front of each subject and an adverb after each verb.

MORE ON MODIFIERS

- **PREPOSITIONAL PHRASE:** The phrase is used to express meanings that cannot be handled by one-word modifiers. For example, we say *We walked by the store* because we cannot say *We walked storely*. The three words *by the store* combine to form a prepositional phrase. It includes a preposition *by* and its object *store*. A preposition joins nouns and pronouns (the objects) to other parts of the sentence. Prepositional phrases can be used as adjectives, adverbs, or nouns. Usually, they show a relation in position (*We fell against the wall.*), direction (*Expenses climbed out of sight.*), and time (*It rained during the evening.*).

- **VERBAL:** A verbal is part verb and part something else— a word used as a noun or adjective.

  ✔ When the other part is used as a noun, the verbal is called a GERUND (*Riding is good exercise.*).

  ✔ When the other part is used as an adjective, the verbal is a PARTICIPLE (*The sleeping watchman snored on.*).

  ✔ Another kind of verbal, the INFINITIVE, is a verb form preceded by the word *to* that can be used as a noun (*To jog is great fun.*) or as an adjective (*The one to see is the manager.*).

WRITE • WRITE • WRITE • WRITE • WRITE • WRITE

Turn to the exercise on the second basic sentence pattern (subject/verb/object). Revise about half of these sentences by adding a prepositional phrase to each. For example: *He shut the door for the last time. He mowed the grass after sunset. In the second edition, he corrected the error.*

Fill the rest of this page with sentences containing verbals— gerunds, participles, and infinitives. Use gerunds and infinitives as subjects and objects in your sentence: *Smoking is prohibited. I enjoy reading. To err is human.* Use participles as adjectives: *The moving car could not be stopped. The yawning girl irritated her supervisor.*

Building Sentences

- To understand sentence structures and types, you must understand what a **CLAUSE** is. It is a group of words that includes a subject and a verb. Clauses are sometimes confused with phrases. A phrase never includes both a subject *and* a verb.

- Clauses are classified as INDEPENDENT or DEPENDENT. If the subject and verb, along with their modifiers, make a complete statement, the clause is called independent —or main. (**Note: every grammatical sentence contains one or more INDEPENDENT clauses.**) If the group of words containing a subject and verb do not make a complete statement, the clause is called dependent—or subordinate.

He opened his box of fishing lures.

  (This sentence contains a subject and verb and makes a complete statement. It is an independent clause.)

When he opened his box of lures.

  (There is a subject and verb, but the statement is incomplete. The word *when* makes the clause dependent.)

35

- All of the sentences you have been writing thus far in the exercises have been simple sentences. **A SIMPLE SENTENCE is composed of one INDEPENDENT clause.** (This is another reasonable definition of a sentence.) Now we will review some other sentence types.

How Sentences Are Classified

- Sentences are classified in two ways: rhetorically and grammatically. (Rhetoric is the art of using words effectively in speaking or writing to persuade or influence.) Rhetorically, sentences are divided into several types: a **DECLARATIVE** sentence makes a statement, an **INTERROGATIVE** one asks a question, an **IMPERATIVE** sentence commands, and an **EXCLAMATORY** one expresses strong feeling.

- The grammatical classification is more useful to writers. Grammatically, sentences are called **SIMPLE, COMPOUND, COMPLEX,** and **COMPOUND-COMPLEX.** The particular classification is based on the kind and number of clauses in the sentence.

  ✔ A SIMPLE SENTENCE contains one independent clause.

  The men fish.

  ✔ A COMPOUND SENTENCE contains two or more independent clauses and no dependent ones.

  I hope, and I pray.

37

✔ A COMPLEX SENTENCE contains one independent clause and one or more dependent clauses.

I detest politicians who lie.

✔ A COMPOUND-COMPLEX SENTENCE contains two or more independent clauses and one or more dependent clauses.

I admire editors who admit mistakes, but I note that I have met few of them.

• Why all these possibilities? For this reason: **Each sentence type is appropriate for an expression of certain ideas.** This relation between sentence structure and the ideas or feelings we want to communicate is critical to writing.

Simple Sentences

- A **SIMPLE SENTENCE** is made up of one independent clause. This clause includes a subject and a verb, either or both of which may be compound (that is, more than one). Simple sentences may vary greatly in length and look anything but simple. Yet when all the elaboration is stripped away, only one clause remains.

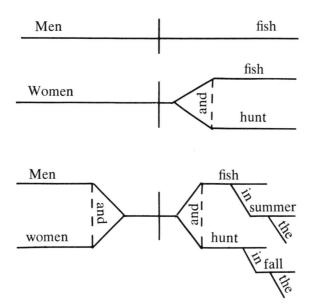

- WHEN DO YOU USE THE SIMPLE SENTENCE? First, there is no better way to untangle your thoughts than to express them in simple sentences. For another use, remember that the short, simple sentence is the most EMPHATIC sentence you write. **The simple sentence calls attention to itself.**

> **EVERY WRITER SHOULD CONSIDER A GREATER, NOT AN EXCLUSIVE, USE OF THE SIMPLE SENTENCE.**

WRITE • WRITE • WRITE • WRITE • WRITE • WRITE

Write a paragraph of eight to ten sentences using only simple sentences. Include compound elements (two or more subjects, verbs, objects, or some combination) as frequently as possible. Be sure that each sentence contains a subject and verb and makes a complete statement. Underline the subjects and verbs.

Compound Sentences

- A **COMPOUND SENTENCE** contains two or more independent clauses but no dependent ones. **The compound sentence shows the connection between ideas.** In a group of simple sentences the reader's attention is drawn in turn to each sentence's statement. In a compound sentence the connected statements are related as parts of a larger idea.

- Use a compound sentence to note a connection, a relationship between two or more statements. This kind of sentence brings together similar ideas that are of equal importance. Such equality is shown below, where the clauses are placed side by side.

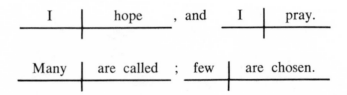

- PUNCTUATE THE COMPOUND SENTENCE CARE-FULLY. When the independent clauses in a compound sentence are joined by one of the coordinating conjunctions (*and, or, nor, but, yet, for*), that conjunction is preceded by a comma. If there is no coordinating conjunction, the correct punctuation mark is a semicolon.

Alcoholism is a health problem, and anyone with this problem should be given the chance to recover.

Alcoholism is a health problem; anyone with this problem should be given the chance to recover.

- So when you think <u>compound</u> you are thinking separation and connection of ideas. **Do not kid yourself about the connection.** The clauses in a compound sentence must be meaningfully related, and this relationship must be pinpointed by the conjunction. Note the various relationships expressed in these compound sentences.

SUPPLEMENTARY: *They argue, and they fight.*

ALTERNATION: *They argue, or they fight.*

CONTRAST: *They argue, but they do not fight.*

CONSEQUENCE: *They started arguing, so they began to fight.*

SEQUENCE: *He started arguing, and the others joined in.*

WRITE • WRITE • WRITE • WRITE • WRITE • WRITE

Write ten compound sentences in each of which you bring together closely related ideas. Try a variety of connections, both punctuation and words like *but, for,* and *or.* In a few compound sentences, include more than two independent clauses. Underline the subjects and verbs.

Complex Sentences

- A **COMPLEX SENTENCE** contains one independent and one or more dependent clauses used as various parts of speech (adjectives, adverbs, or nouns). After the simple sentence, the complex is the most useful to writers. This kind of sentence enables a writer TO SHOW THE RELATIVE IMPORTANCE OF IDEAS, TO QUALIFY A STATEMENT, and TO DEFINE THOUGHTS PRECISELY.

- **The function of a complex sentence is to subordinate ideas.** Every complex sentence says to a reader, "Here is the important idea in the independent clause, and here is a related but less important idea in the dependent clause." The writer's job is to select the words and arrange the ideas so as to define this relationship exactly.

- **The main idea of a complex sentence must appear in the INDEPENDENT clause; the less important one(s) in the DEPENDENT clause(s).** The mixture of unequal ideas typical of complex sentences is reflected in these diagrams:

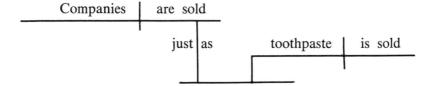

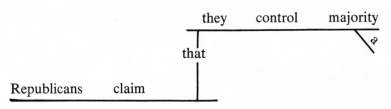

NOTE how each dependent clause is used as a single part of speech—in the first example as an adverb, in the second as a noun.

- The dependent clauses in complex sentences are usually introduced by relative pronouns (*who, which, that,* etc.), or subordinating conjunctions (like *since, although, because*). Such connections are decisive in defining relationships.

> <u>*After*</u> *he saw the police car, he speeded up.*

> <u>*Because*</u> *he saw the police car, he speeded up.*

> <u>*Although*</u> *he saw the police car, he speeded up.*

WRITE • WRITE • WRITE • WRITE • WRITE • WRITE

Write a dozen complex sentences, each with a different relative pronoun or subordinating conjunction introducing the dependent clause. Underline the subjects and verbs in both the independent and the dependent clauses.

Compound-Complex Sentences

- The **COMPOUND-COMPLEX** sentence contains two or more independent clauses with one or more clauses dependent on them.

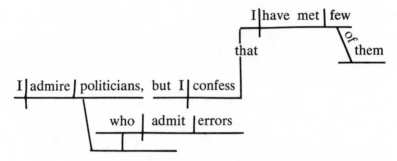

Life is complicated enough without the piled-up confusion of compound-complex sentences. Use the simpler sentence types.

Touchstones for Writing Effective Sentences

● Suppose you wanted to combine the ideas of two sentences: *The man was desperate. The man reached for a gun.* Here are some possible combinations:

> *The man was desperate, and he reached for a gun.*
> *Because the man was desperate, he reached for a gun.*
> *The man who was desperate reached for a gun.*
> *The man who reached for a gun was desperate.*
> *Desperate, the man reached for a gun.*
> *The desperate man reached for a gun.*
> *A gun was reached for by the desperate man.*
> *The man reached for a gun when he was desperate.*
> *The man reaching for a gun was desperate.*

All of these sentences—simple, compound, and complex—have the same core of meaning about the desperate man. But each differs from all the others. It is easy to see why writers can be overwhelmed at times with the choices at their disposal. Which is the most effective sentence? Is one better than the others? How can you be sure you have selected the best sentence construction?

49

- The truth is that there are few certainties in the writing process. You are never sure you have the perfect form for the meaning you want to express. Nevertheless, there are some clues. The context of your total thought, the emphasis desired, the audience: all of these will help you determine the best arrangement of word, phrase, and clause. Keep in mind these touchstones for writing effective sentences:

✔ SAY SOMETHING SIGNIFICANT. Your first check is to be certain that your idea or feeling is worth writing about. Do not waste time trying to improve something that was not there to begin with.

✔ SELECT THE APPROPRIATE SENTENCE STRUCTURE. Remember that one sentence structure (simple, compound, or complex) is especially appropriate for the thought you want to write. Find it!

✔ ARRANGE WORDS FOR EMPHASIS. You took care of part of the chore when you selected a sentence structure. Be sure that the emphasis you want shows. Do not bury important points.

✔ KEEP SENTENCES SHORT. To ensure reader comprehension, check that your sentences are typically short— rarely more than 20–25 words. Use only what is necessary.

✔ ONE IDEA TO A SENTENCE. Break your thought into small blocks of meaning. Limit yourself when possible to one idea to a sentence. Do not overload your sentences.

- Sentences are the critical element of your writing. Your thinking and your language merge here or nowhere. The process of writing effective sentences is demanding. It is check and recheck. It is change and change again. That is what good writing is all about. **WRITE. CHECK. REVISE. WRITE. CHECK. REVISE.**

PARAGRAPHS

Paragraphs

- **WRITING PARAGRAPHS IS NOT SO DIFFERENT FROM WRITING SENTENCES.** When you write a sentence, you start with a subject and verb and refine your statement with modifiers. With a paragraph, you also start with a subject (topic) and refine it with modifiers that are complete sentences. The process of defining and describing your idea is the same. With paragraphs, the writing unit is simply larger.

- A paragraph is a collection of related sentences dealing with a single subject. So reads the usual definition. But paragraphs come in all shapes and sizes, and they serve many purposes. THINK OF PARAGRAPHS AS A KIND OF PUNCTUATION. We break our thoughts into paragraphs to make easier going for our readers.

- If you think paragraphs are unimportant, imagine the front page of your daily newspaper without them. You can bet that you would have to read much more slowly. Printers say that paragraphs give "air" to a page. They provide a reader some breathing space so that he is not overwhelmed by the mass of words.

- PARAGRAPHING IS ANOTHER MEANS OF LEADING OUR READERS STEP BY STEP THROUGH OUR

NOT-ALWAYS-LOGICAL THOUGHT PROCESSES. Every time we indent we are saying to a reader, "Here's a part of my writing I want you to see as a unit. Here's a block of my meaning." What is important is that we have alerted the reader. When he sees that indentation, he is primed for the next phase of our subject.

- Now we must deliver. The paragraph must make a point. IT MUST JUSTIFY ITSELF AS A UNIT. There should be no question why this group of sentences was labelled a paragraph.

How To Build a Paragraph

- We are concerned here with the **MECHANICS OF PARA-GRAPH BUILDING.** For this purpose, we assume the writer has a subject and a content that must now be arranged in paragraphs. Later, we will look at the problem of developing a subject and its content.

- IN ANY PIECE OF WRITING THERE SHOULD BE MOVEMENT. A thought goes from somewhere to somewhere else—or the reader is wasting his time. Moreover, the reader should be able to follow that movement. Fortunately, there are some easy and obvious ways to arrange material within paragraphs.

- MOST PARAGRAPHS ARE BUILT AROUND A COMBINATION OF SPECIFIC DETAIL AND GENERAL STATEMENTS. Essentially, the writer's organizing problem is: Which comes first in the paragraph, the detail or the statement? The writer can (1) begin with a general statement and then supply the necessary detail or (2) begin with the detail and lead up to a general statement at the end of the paragraph. In other words, the two **logical ways of organizing** are to move from **the general to the specific** or from **the specific to the general.**

57

GENERAL ——→SPECIFIC

This is the most useful method of organizing. You can begin with a general statement—your concept of what the paragraph is all about. Next comes a series of sentences containing the supporting facts that explain and clarify the general statement. Finally, there can be a wrap-up sentence for any necessary summary.

> *Business Administration has become one of the most popular majors at American colleges and universities. At private colleges like Colby and Trinity, 22% of last year's junior class selected this major, up from 16% three years ago. A record 33% of state university juniors did the same. Columbia's business dean says these students relish the practical experience of many business courses and the prospect of good starting salaries.*

- Since most paragraphs are elaborations of a general statement, you have only to follow the implications of that lead sentence to develop a paragraph. If the statement is a DEFINITION, the paragraph will define with detail and examples. If you are describing a PROCESS, you will explain each step of the process in turn. If you are taking a side in an ARGUMENT, the paragraph will present the detail (in order of importance) that supports your position.

SPECIFIC ⟶ GENERAL

This method of arranging detail and generalization permits the writer to catch the reader's attention with interesting detail and to prepare him for the general statement at the end. This arrangement is also known as a climax paragraph.

> *Fifteen years from now every man, woman, and child in these United States will have to wear some kind of breathing helmet to survive outdoors. Most of our animals and much of our plant life will be dead. We will look out of our sealed windows at deserted streets. In twenty-five years, man will live in domed cities. Today, we are destroying our atmosphere, and our future is inevitable.*

- So much for the LOGICAL methods of organizing material. There are two other equally useful NATURAL methods of arranging detail within a paragraph:

- **CHRONOLOGICAL ORDER:** If you were called upon to write a brief report on your week's work, you would be well advised to arrange your account chronologically. In the first sentence you could tell what happened on Monday, the second and third might take care of Tuesday, and so on through the week. The chronological order can handle any amount, and practically any kind, of material.

> *Monday is the most difficult day for me in the mailroom. On that day, I receive the largest number of first-class letters to be routed. Usually, that number is more than three times*

as many as for any other day. I expect to spend all day Monday and Tuesday and part of Wednesday routing this mail. Since there is a big drop-off on Tuesday, I am able to catch up by Wednesday. The Thursday and Friday incoming mail presents no problem for me to handle.

SPATIAL ORDER: At times you will want to describe what you see in terms of spatial relationships. That is, if you are describing a static scene, do it in a regular sequence—from left to right, top to bottom, near to far. Do not jump around. Keep your reader's eye moving in a consistent sweep.

The heavy growth of trees and shrubs, as well as the irregular roof line, hides the fact this is a very long house—over 125 feet. On the left, looking from north to south, one sees that a darkly painted garage and kitchen account for one-third of the length. In the center, framed in a light-textured wood exterior, are the dining and living room areas. On the right, almost hidden in some towering hemlocks, is the original barn structure now used as a studio and sleeping quarters.

WRITE • WRITE • WRITE • WRITE • WRITE • WRITE

(1) Make a list of ten to twelve actions or roles you must perform in a typical work day. Jot them down as they come to mind.

(2) When you have a list, rearrange the items into a chronological order that is close to the actual time in which they are performed in your work day.

(3) Next, rearrange the items into the order of their importance to your job. The most important actions or roles should come first.

(4) Finally, write a paragraph of eight to ten sentences on the subject of your job—what you do. Begin with a general statement and then support it with a series of sentences that includes relevant detail in either chronological order or order of importance.

The Content of Paragraphs

- **CONTENT IS PRIMARY:** With all deference to style and form, punctuation and grammar, a paragraph finally stands or falls on its content—on the importance of what the writer has to say. If the reader judges the content worth his time and memory, the writing is successful. If the reader skims and finally stops reading, the writing has failed. This is what content is all about.

- CONTENT REFLECTS THE WRITER'S THOUGHT PROCESS. The writer edits his thinking into a content that will mean something to a reader. One way is to reconstruct the several stages in the thought process that originally produced the idea or scene he wants to write about. For example, if you wanted to argue for or against gun control, you could review the reasons that convinced you of the soundness of your position. You have to pull these reasons out of your memory, juggle them, and mentally arrange them in the order of their importance. Such a list could become the first draft of the content that will appear in your paper on gun control.

- STRIVE FOR A BALANCE OF FACTS AND GENER- ALIZATIONS. In all writing there is an interplay of facts (details, images, etc.) and generalizations (ideas, opinions, judgments, etc.), with each supporting the other. There must be a balance. Facts can be used to "cow" readers; generalizations to "bull" them. We need generalizations to clarify the significance of facts, just as we need facts to make our generalizations convincing.

- As a final word: content should call attention to the IMPORTANCE OF DETAIL—THE VITALITY OF THE FACT. Unfortunately for most of us, the vague and weary generalization comes more quickly to mind than the convincing, picture-making fact. **Search out the factual detail to which a reader can relate.** Note the detail in the following description:

You can't say much for a landscape that fails to attract one of Americans' favorite birds: the hummingbird. A tiny bird, rarely more than four inches long, "hummers" are admired for their magnificent colors (brilliant reds, iridescent oranges, metallic greens) and for their aerial acrobatics. They hover, they dart, they dive, they even fly backwards! Their constant state of animation requires tremendous energy, and so their food needs are no less gigantic. Some birders estimate that a hummer consumes more than half its weight in sugar each day.

Transition Techniques

- In an effective paragraph all the sentences are tied together in a coherent whole. This coherence exists in the ideas; it is not a quality that can be mechanically added in revision. Nevertheless, it is the writer's responsibility to make this coherence as evident as possible with certain transition techniques. **TRANSITIONAL WORDS, PHRASES, AND DEVICES ARE USED TO TIE SENTENCES TOGETHER, TO SPELL OUT RELATIONSHIPS, AND TO MAKE POINTS APPARENT.**

- Three transition techniques are especially useful:

  (1) REPEAT KEY WORDS/PHRASES to tie sentences together.

    For some the course will be a review, _for_ others an introduction. _For_ all the course sets an achievable standard.

  (2) USE A PRONOUN to refer to a word (its antecedent) in the preceding sentence.

64

The Navy will spend $100 million to return three battleships to service. They will be used in the Mediterranean.

(3) USE TRANSITIONAL EXPRESSIONS like *besides, finally, afterwards, however, for example, of course, on the other hand,* and many more to tie the parts of a paragraph together.

For one thing, continuing Near East tensions have made some of the Arab countries more receptive to an American presence in the area. Moreover, new administrations in the U.S. and Israel may bring on new peace talks. In addition, the moderate countries in the Arab world have a stronger voice.

Paragraph Length

- How long should a paragraph be? There are no inflexible rules. **THE RIGHT LENGTH DEPENDS ON THE SUBJECT, PURPOSE IN WRITING, AUDIENCE, AND READING CONVENTIONS.**

- Note some of these conventions. Newspaper paragraphs are typically short (20–40 words), the right length for quick reading. Paragraphs in popular magazines range from 100–150 words; in nonfiction books, from 125–250 words.

- Do not count the words in your paragraphs. Instead, as you write, TRY TO VISUALIZE YOUR FINAL ASSORTMENT OF PARAGRAPHS.

  ✔ If you spot a run of short paragraphs, check for adequate development of ideas within these paragraphs.

  ✔ If you come up with a very long paragraph (a page or more), consider breaking it up for easier reading.

  ✔ Try to vary paragraph lengths. Follow a long one with a short one. VARIETY DESTROYS MONOTONY AND CREATES INTEREST.

66

WRITE • WRITE • WRITE • WRITE • WRITE • WRITE

Rewrite the paragraph you wrote in the last exercise, focusing on an improved content and coherence (transitions). Make the content as specific and as factual as possible. Try to make all parts of your paragraph hang together in a coherent whole by a judicious use of transition techniques.

WRITING PROCEDURE

Writing Procedure

- Paragraphs, chapters, books: ALL ARE WRITTEN AC-CORDING TO THE SAME PRINCIPLES. You put several paragraphs together just as you construct a single one. In both instances, the writer must pinpoint a subject, plan its delivery, and then write and revise. In this section we have brought together some of the principles in a **Writing Procedure** that will be useful in all your writing assignments.

- In any writing, whether it be a short letter or a long book, a writer goes through four distinct stages:

    1. PRELIMINARY THINKING

    2. PLANNING

    3. WRITING

    4. REVISING

- Depending on the size of the writing effort, the writer may spend minutes or months in any of these stages. But he must spend time in each of them if he wants to write effectively.

- Most important to recognize is the fact that there are two stages—THINKING and PLANNING—to be reckoned with before one worries about the actual writing. Most of us rush into the writing stage without thinking long enough about what we want to say, without a plan for how we want to say it. Why? Because it is easier to write than to think about writing.

CLEAR, EFFECTIVE WRITING IS THE RESULT OF SERIOUS THINKING AND CAREFUL PLANNING.

Stage 1 — Preliminary Thinking

- Ideas for writing usually come easily enough. The difficulty begins when we try to translate the idea into the words, sentences, and paragraphs that will mean something to a reader.

- Your first concern should be to see the possibilities and the limitations of the idea you may write about. The most critical question: **IS THE IDEA WORTH WRITING ABOUT?** To answer it, examine the idea from three angles: from YOUR OWN POINT OF VIEW, from the angle of CONTENT, and from THE READER'S POINT OF VIEW.

- YOUR POINT OF VIEW: Pinpoint the idea. Usually this is a matter of cutting it down to size. Does it still interest you after you have limited it? Do you think others will be interested?

- THE CONTENT: Look as objectively as possible at the facts and details that give preliminary form to your idea. Are there enough facts and details? Are they interesting? If you have difficulty pinpointing specific material, recreate the train of circumstances that led you to the idea. Do you see a tentative order in the content? If you are planning an argument, do some reasons stand out as more important than others? If you intend to write about an event, is the chronological framework apparent? At this stage you are trying to judge the adequacy of your content.

- THE READER'S POINT OF VIEW: Who is going to read your paper? Once you define that audience, you can try to gauge its response to your idea. Will this audience be interested in the idea you want to write about? Would they agree or disagree with you? Does it matter?

- DO NOT RUSH THIS STAGE. When you think that you are ready to move on, try to draft a single sentence that contains your main idea. This **main idea sentence** is a kind of proposition. It states the main objective of the writing you have in mind, the most important point you plan to make. This sentence can be the touchstone to which you refer as you write. **It is your working sketch.** Here, for example, is the main idea sentence of this book:

  Writing skills are the result of a mastery of the following elements and techniques: specific subjects and action verbs; short, simple sentences; paragraphs as the writing unit; transitional words and phrases; and exhaustive revision.

- Not until you have written down and accepted the main idea sentence are you ready to move on to the planning stage.

WRITE • WRITE • WRITE • WRITE • WRITE • WRITE

In the next four exercises you will be working your way through the four writing stages. The end product will be a writing sample of several paragraphs (about 500 words) in which you examine one of the following topics:

✔ An analysis of your present job, your school or college program, or your career goals.

✔ An argument about environmental protection: do we need more or less?

✔ A persuasive article on TV programming (see page 93).

✔ A discussion of some aspects of your hobby or favorite sport.

Your immediate purpose in this exercise is to select one of these topics and take it through the thinking stage up to the formulation of a main idea sentence.

Review the commentary on Stage 1 and apply it to the topic that interests you. If the suggestions do not work for you, try some other approaches. Jot down the words and phrases that reflect your mind in action as it attempts to focus on a subject. Fill a page with these impressions.

Finally, when you think you have a topic, write out the main idea sentence. Read it and reread it. Change it as often as necessary. Check it out from your own point of view ("Do I have a good grasp of what I want to say?"), from the angle of content ("Does there appear to be an adequate content?

Will I have enough to say?"), and, most importantly, from the reader's point of view ("Will what I have to say interest a reader?").

Write your draft of the main idea sentence. It is your working sketch as you move into the planning stage.

Stage 2 — Planning

- Once you have a main idea sentence, you are coming out of the groping stage. You have a subject. The problem now is to deliver that subject to a reader. **THAT IS WHAT PLANNING IS ALL ABOUT: HOW TO DIRECT A READER'S RESPONSE TO A PARTICULAR END—TO AN ACCEPTANCE OF YOUR MAIN IDEA.**

- You know something about the several ways you can arrange material in a paragraph. You can use the same LOGICAL and NATURAL methods to organize more than one paragraph. The choice depends in part on the subject and the reader. If you are analyzing your present job or arguing about the environment or TV programming, you might well list details in the order of their importance. For a discussion of your career plans, you would be more apt to use a chronological order.

- Planning permits you to be sure that when you start writing you know where you are going and where you are stopping. **Use any planning technique that works for you:** outlines, scratch notes, lists, cards, whatever. Use any method that allows for errors of judgment, for continuing criticism, and for getting rid of useless information. **YOU CANNOT DO THIS PLANNING IN YOUR HEAD.**

Although **OUTLINE** is a dirty word to many writers, you cannot beat it for usefulness. It is one sound method of planning:

- Read and reread the main idea sentence, probing for all its implications.

- On 3″ × 5″ cards (they are easy to juggle), write all the topics suggested by the main idea sentence. Use one card for each topic. You want to see what you have to work with.

- Read each of the topics and put any related ones together in a pile of their own. You should begin to see some main groupings and some of lesser importance.

- Organize the piles according to some natural or logical order. Use the same organizing scheme within each pile.

- Once you have an order for the main groupings, you have your outline. Write it down. This is your working plan. Keep in mind, however, that no plan is carved in stone. You may—you should—change it for any good reason at any stage of the writing process.

WRITE • WRITE • WRITE • WRITE • WRITE • WRITE

The goal of this exercise is a fully developed plan. You can use any technique you want. Read and reread the main idea sentence and then list (in words and phrases) all the parts/divisions/ideas/details that come to mind as the kind of material you want to include. The next step is to select one of the logical (general⟶specific, specific⟶general) or natural (chronological, spatial) orders as your organizing method. Finally, write out your plan in as much detail as you can.

Stage 3 — Writing

- Your task in this FIRST AND ROUGH DRAFT is to flesh out your outline, to get your story told. Your concern is not with appearance or fine phrasing or impeccable grammar. **YOUR CHIEF MOTIVATION IN THIS DRAFT IS TO GET YOUR LINE OF THOUGHT DOWN ON PAPER.** You can dress it up later.

- With your main idea sentence and your plan before you as guides, start writing. Plunge into your subject. Pick out some important detail, something that interests you, and take off. TRY TO CATCH A FLOW OF THOUGHT. Write rapidly. Write as much as possible of this first draft without stopping. If you run out of words, return to your plan. The blank pages often fill up quickly with this technique.

- **SOME TIPS ON GETTING STARTED:**

  ✔ JUST START. Write the word "The" as soon as you sit down. A noun and verb, hopefully, will follow.

  ✔ LOOK AROUND. Describe something you see—a view, a photograph. Ease into your real subject.

✔ PICK A WORD related to your subject. Look it up in your dictionary.

✔ SET UP AN IMAGINARY READER. What would she want to know?

✔ Remember that every piece of writing has a beginning, middle, and end. Your plan takes care of the middle. Use the beginning to tell how important your subject is, the end to summarize or draw conclusions.

WRITE • WRITE • WRITE • WRITE • WRITE • WRITE

Write the rough draft of the subject you defined and planned in the previous two exercises. Write rapidly and as much as possible at one sitting. Your objective is to get the story told, to reach the end. Follow the plan you prepared in the second stage. If it does not work, revise it, make a new one, and start over. Do not try to muddle along with a patchwork.

Stage 4 — Revising

- **GOOD WRITING IS NEARLY ALWAYS REVISED WRITING.** Unfortunately, it is difficult to convince inexperienced writers of the importance of revision. Most of us are so relieved to have filled a page with any kind of words that we do not want to tamper with the accomplishment. The truth is that **most first drafts are an editorial embarrassment.** They are inexact in their word choice, vague in their detail, and rambling in their thought development.

- **ASK A PROFESSIONAL WRITER ABOUT HIS REVISION PRACTICES.** The professionals know the pain of revision. They know what it is to rewrite an opening sentence a dozen or more times—and still not be satisfied with it. DISCIPLINE and STAMINA are as much a part of the writing process as grammar and punctuation.

- **ATTITUDE IS THE CRUX.** Unless you are convinced that revision is indispensable to the writing process, you will not reach your potential as a writer. At this point you can ease yourself into the revision habit. By skipping lines so as to leave room for changes, by writing clearly and openly, you can make the critical assumption that THIS IS A FIRST

DRAFT and that you will be working it over. That is half the revision battle.

- **WHERE TO BEGIN?** At some moment you will come to what you think is the end of your first draft. Now you must confront it. You know it is not in final form; you know there must be changes and corrections. The possibilities are many. For openers, you might condense, or expand, or start over. Revision, as part of the editorial process, involves two considerations:

   1. THE CONTENT AND CLARITY OF YOUR WRITING, and

   2. ITS CORRECTNESS AND APPROPRIATENESS.

- **CONTENT AND CLARITY:** Content is fundamental. Unless you have something worth your reader's time and concentration, nothing else matters very much. If you do have something worthwhile to say, the next matter of importance is the clarity with which you express yourself. If a reader does not know what you are talking about, your ship is sinking. The following questions will help you focus on these two important considerations.

   1. Is your main idea clearly stated or implied somewhere in your writing? Underline the statement or indicate where it is implied.

   2. What do you want your readers to remember when they finish reading? Do you take advantage of the opportunity afforded by your first and last paragraphs to emphasize your objectives in writing?

3. What is the overall order in which you present your material? Is it a logical or a natural scheme?

4. What about the amount of supporting detail? Too little or too much? Which is the strongest paragraph in your paper? Why?

5. Would you characterize your content as factual or general? Is the content appropriate for your audience?

6. Underline the key transitional devices in your paper. Are they adequate to lead a reader along your line of thought?

- **CORRECTNESS AND APPROPRIATENESS:** Reread the first draft for mechanical errors and faults on three levels: paragraph, sentence, and word.

PARAGRAPH ORGANIZATION:

1. Is the main idea apparent in each paragraph? Does every detail in a paragraph relate to its central idea?

2. Does each paragraph have an obvious scheme for ordering its materials?

3. Is it easy to follow the line of thought in each paragraph? Does one sentence lead logically into the next? Underline and evaluate each of the transitional devices. Would additional ones help your readers?

4. What about the length of each paragraph? Too long or too short?

SENTENCE STRUCTURE:

1. Does each sentence have a subject, a verb, a complete idea? Underline the subjects and verbs. Are the subjects specific? Are the verbs action verbs?

2. Does each sentence say something that is worth saying? Is the meaning apparent on first reading? Do you hold to the principle of one idea to a sentence?

3. Do your important ideas stand out in the right places? Have you emphasized them to your advantage? Is the main idea in the main clause of each complex sentence? Did you remember that first and last are the most emphatic positions?

4. Is each sentence punctuated correctly? Check compound sentences carefully for comma splices. (See the *Guide to Grammar and Punctuation.*)

5. What about grammatical errors—dangling modifiers, non-agreement of subject and verb, pronoun references? (See the *Guide.*)

6. Take a second look at any sentence that runs on and on. Short is better.

WORD CHOICE:

1. Overall, is the choice of words appropriate to your readers?

2. Are you using a big or formal word where a simple one could do the job? Be natural.

3. Are you using strong, active verbs that make your writing move?

WRITE • WRITE • WRITE • WRITE • WRITE • WRITE

Revise the rough draft you wrote in the previous exercise. Read and reread the draft until you have a sharp impression of its content, clarity, correctness, and appropriateness. Write your final draft.

Some Familiar Writing Forms

The **WRITING PROCEDURE** will see you through most of your writing assignments. There is no writing chore, whether it be a letter to the editor or a technical manual, that will not profit from thinking and planning, that will not improve with each revision. Nevertheless, there are some additional editorial suggestions to be made about three of the most familiar writing forms: business letters, persuasive articles, and term papers.

Business Letters

You have an important letter to write. You are applying for a job. You need an appointment with a company buyer. You want to complain or plead or deny or claim. How do you write an effective business letter?

- The first and best advice is to **KEEP YOUR EYE ON THE WRITING.** Do not let yourself get trapped by the mechanics of letter writing. Of course, the letter should be typed; of course, it should be neat; of course, it should be signed legibly. Select one of the following formats (or any other reasonable, consistent arrangement) and forget it. Concentrate on the writing.

- All of the writing guidelines—**THINK, PLAN, WRITE,** and **REVISE**—should come into play in writing the business letter. Be especially concerned about the pre-writing stages of thinking and planning. WHAT DO YOU WANT TO SAY? WHY SPECIFICALLY ARE YOU WRITING THIS LETTER? Your ability to frame a main idea sentence is the best evidence that you know where you are going.

- **STATE YOUR PURPOSE IN THE OPENING PARA-GRAPH.** Let there be no doubt about why you are writing. Begin with a clear statement of your purpose. If you are answering a letter, refer to its date.

- In the body of your letter, use the plan (outline) you have developed. You will probably be organizing your material with one of the logical orders, but there will be many occasions when the chronological order will be appropriate. **KEEP THE READER IN MIND.** Your letter will be successful in accordance with your ability to anticipate your reader's interests and needs.

- **BE NATURAL.** Avoid the jargon of so many business letters. ("Yours of the 29th at hand." "I remain yours respectfully.") You would never use such phrases in direct speech. Skip the phony formalities. Write simply, clearly, and naturally. The guideline about specific subjects and action verbs will stand you in good stead here.

- In the final paragraph, **MAKE CLEAR THE ACTION YOU DESIRE.** If you want an appointment, say so. If you expect an order, make it easy for him to give you one. If you need a letter of recommendation, ask for it. Leave as little as possible to chance interpretation.

- Revise as often as necessary to make your letter **PERFECT.**

Persuasive Articles

In one sense most writing is persuasive in nature. Certainly, we want our readers to accept our treatment of a topic. But usually our first purpose is to inform or to explain. A persuasive article, on the other hand, has a different purpose. It not only discusses an issue but takes a position on it. It offers an opinion, a preference, a judgment. The first purpose of a persuasive article is to convince readers that what we say is true—that our opinion, our preference, our judgment is the right one.

- A persuasive article/paper has two parts: **THESIS** ("what") and **PROOF** ("why"). The thesis is the issue, the central belief or action that the writer proposes to his readers. The proof is the evidence the writer puts up in support of his position.

- In selecting a thesis, **STICK TO YOUR EXPERIENCE AND READING.** The best topic for you is the one about which you have both INFORMATION and CONVICTION.

- **HOW TO PERSUADE?** What do we do when we try to persuade someone to accept our proposition? Briefly, we use reasons. We claim that a certain statement is true, and to "prove" that it is, we give reasons. These reasons are our evidence, our proof. I might try to convince you that the next president will be a woman. I offer my reasons (evidence). Whether you believe me or not depends on whether you find the evidence convincing.

- **LOGIC IS YOUR MOST PERSUASIVE TECHNIQUE FOR PRESENTING EVIDENCE,** the logic that evolves from study and analysis. You touched on logic in our discussion of organizing methods: the interplay of detail and generalization. In attempting to persuade someone by moving from detail (facts or reasons) to generalization, you resort to an INDUCTIVE METHOD OF REASONING. When you move from generalization to detail, it is a DEDUCTIVE METHOD OF REASONING.

- **INDUCTIVE REASONING:** Here the initial appeal is to facts, to an experience one can test with one's senses. The writer begins by saying something about a particular event (John Wayne's mortality) and he adds other facts (John Lennon's mortality) and on the basis of these he arrives at the generalization that "All men are mortal." The facts cited are the reasons for the truth of the generalization. Many kinds of statements can be proved or disproved by personal observation ("Last Saturday, lightning hit the Hanovers' house."), by appeals to experience ("Most wars are followed by inflationary periods."), and by facts ("The hostages spent 444 days in captivity."). HANDLE INDUCTIVE REASONING WITH CARE. It is easy to misrepresent evidence, to jump too quickly to generalizations, to use questionable authorities.

- **DEDUCTIVE REASONING:** In reasoning deductively the writer begins with statements that he knows or believes are true. He then uses these statements to move to others. Often, this process is enough to prove that the other statements are true. The reader accepts their truth because the first ones are true. Suppose you "know" that all salesmen in XYZ Company are under fifty years of age. This is the first statement. Now what statement can you move to? One possibility is that salesman A is under fifty. You do not have to ask him or check any records. All you or your reader has to know is that the first statement is true. This process is called deductive reasoning. If we are justified in moving from the first statement, then we say that the second statement follows from the first (or the first implies the second).

> **NOTE: There are some complex rules for applying the deductive formula (that is, syllogisms). Most standard composition books discuss the procedures in detail.**

Finally, it is the **QUALITY OF YOUR EVIDENCE** that determines how persuasive your argument will be. Evidence is factual. Once again, we come to the PRIMACY OF THE FACT as the secret of effective writing.

Term Papers

Earlier and earlier in their school years, students are being introduced to the term paper assignment. By the time they reach high school, they are handling footnotes and bibliographies with few second thoughts. There is no need to repeat here the mechanics of term paper preparation. Instead we will look to some matters that are easily lost sight of in writing long papers.

- "Term" paper is an unfortunate tag. It sounds like prison jargon. Prefer to think of it as a **RESEARCH** paper. It is research into a project that interests you; it is original research that you must communicate clearly, correctly, and effectively to a reader. Such an effort is far more important to you than a collection of correctly punctuated footnotes.

- There are at least four requisites of a good research paper: (1) a clear discussion of the topic's significance, (2) accurate facts gained from adequate research, (3) sound reasoning, and (4) effective writing.

- **BEWARE OF RESEARCH PAPER STYLE.** Why do so many of us put on our most formal manner when we write this paper? Why do our words and sentences get longer and longer? Forget the jargon. Relax. Be natural. Write as simply and clearly as you can. And as long as neither clarity nor necessary content is sacrificed, SHORTER IS BETTER.

- **USE QUOTATIONS SPARINGLY:** Fight the inclination to include long quotations. When you are about to quote, stop and ask yourself if you could not adequately summarize the idea in less space. Get in the habit of rewriting in your own words.

- **FOOTNOTES ARE FOR USE,** not to prove you have done your homework. There is a student superstition that the quality of research is somehow related to the number of footnotes. Of course, include any footnote that serves a reader—that informs him or directs him. But forget the others.

- **SAVE THE BEGINNING FOR THE END.** Many of us find it difficult at the outset to do justice to the introduction to a research paper. Understandably, we are probably in a better position to write the introduction after we have written the body of the paper. Fine. Write it at the end. You will know at that point exactly where you are going and what you want to emphasize.

- **ORGANIZE!** There is no way you are going to write an effective research paper without a sure direction. Your argument must move—soundly, steadily, convincingly. PLAN, PLAN, PLAN.

ONE MORE TIME

One More Time

- Writing is a natural act, one that can be easily grasped by any speaker of the English language.

- Nine times out of ten what sounds right to you will turn out to be correct grammar.

- No matter how correct it may be in its grammar and punctuation, the real test of a piece of writing is the ease with which it communicates its meaning to readers.

- The first requirement of a good sentence is that it says something worthwhile.

- The subject and verb—the *thing* and the *doing*—are the most important parts of every sentence for this reason: they carry the critical meaning.

- The simple sentence is the key to effective writing: a simple sentence with a concrete subject-doer and an action verb that moves an idea. Subject and verb, idea and comment: that is what a sentence is all about. And that is what the paragraph, the report, and the book are all about.

- The short simple sentence is the most emphatic sentence you write.

- When you think "compound" sentence, you are thinking about separation and connection of ideas.

- Subordination is the business of complex sentences.

- If you want to deliver your word to a reader clearly and quickly, there is no more authoritative advice than to limit yourself to one idea to a sentence.

- Modification—adjectives, adverbs, phrases, and verbals— is a kind of commentary on the subject you are trying to define for your readers.

- One of the best ways to make your writing easy to read and understand is to break your thoughts into small blocks of meaning.

- Think of paragraphing as punctuation.

- Use the actual time-frame to tell what happened first, second, third. Nothing could be easier to write—and to read.

- You will not go wrong if you build most of your paragraphs on the deductive principle. You can open with the general statement. Next comes a series of sentences containing the supporting facts. . . . Finally, there is a wrap-up sentence. . . .

- We need generalizations to clarify the significance of facts, just as we need facts to make our generalizations convincing.

- Revision is an inescapable and indispensable part of the writing process.

In one sentence: writing skills are the result of a mastery of the following elements and techniques: specific subjects and action verbs; short, simple sentences; paragraphs as the writing unit; transitional words and phrases; and exhaustive revision.

At this point you know how to put some basic sentence patterns together and to arrange them logically or chronologically in a paragraph. You also know you would be wise to spend less time writing and more time planning and revising.

That is really all you need to know. The rest is practice.

A GUIDE
TO
GRAMMAR AND
PUNCTUATION

A Guide To Grammar and Punctuation

A grammar book tells us how language works. At least, the good ones do. In school, in one of your English books, you came across a section labelled "Grammar." You may have thought that was "the word" on language. It was not. It was one writer's view of the way language works.

There is no single, definitive grammar of the English language. In fact, there is a wide choice of interpretations. Two of the most respected historical and traditional grammars are Otto Jespersen's seven-volume *A Modern English Grammar on Historical Principles* and George Curme's *A Grammar of the English Language*. But no high school or college English course teaches these. What you see in the typical handbook of English is an adaptation and a summary.

Grammar is a useful tool of a writer—whether he knows it from instinct or study. We do not belittle this instinct for what is correct and what is not. Nevertheless, if one's writing is ever to be a confident activity, one must have resources other than instinct. The writer should know enough about grammar to understand how language works. She can acquire this understanding with not too much effort, without too thick a review volume. A review of the following elements will satisfy most grammatical needs. The list is quite brief.

- **Parts of speech**

- **Phrases**

- **Clauses**

- **Sentences**

- **Agreement**

- **Punctuation**

- **Spelling**

These are the language mechanics you will need to be familiar with in your writing.

Words

The English language contains more than a half million words. Fortunately, all of them can be classified according to the way they are used in a sentence. This classifying scheme we call parts of speech.

Parts of Speech

English has eight parts of speech. Every word we use in our writing can be classified as one of these eight:

- noun
- pronoun
- verb
- adjective

- adverb
- preposition
- conjunction
- interjection

A noun or a pronoun is the thing we want to talk about; a verb expresses action or states of being; adjectives describe things; adverbs describe actions; prepositions and conjunctions make connections; and interjections express surprise or emotion.

An easy way to remember the parts of speech is to collect them functionally:

STATEMENT WORDS   :   NOUNS, PRONOUNS, VERBS

MODIFYING WORDS   :   ADJECTIVES, ADVERBS

CONNECTING WORDS   :   PREPOSITIONS, CONJUNCTIONS

INDEPENDENT WORDS   :   INTERJECTIONS

A word can be finally classified as a particular part of speech only by its use in a specific sentence. The same word can be used as several different parts of speech. For example, the word *fish* can be a noun (*The fish swam away.*) or a verb (*We fish that stream every spring.*) or an adjective (*They sat down to a fish dinner.*).

Here is a longer look at each of the parts of speech.

NOUN: A noun is the name of a person, place, thing, or idea that a sentence talks about. Its basic function is to name something. There are two types of nouns: *common* nouns name classes of persons, places, things, or ideas (*woman, cities, airplane, liberty*); *proper* nouns name a particular person, place, or thing and are always capitalized (*Robert Burns, New Haven, Yale*).

The possessive form of nouns is formed by adding 's to the base word: *the woman's pocketbook, the man's briefcase, the singer's music.* The possessive plural is formed by adding the apostrophe after the final s: *the ladies' hats, the teachers' strike.* But: *the men's tickets,* because *men* is plural.

PRONOUN: Pronouns are little words like *you, me, who, them,* and *someone.* They have varied and often confusing forms. We could spend much time on their details, but you only have to know two things about pronouns early in your writing career. (Later you can check one of the grammar books for pronoun complexity.) First, you should know that we use pronouns so that we do not have to repeat nouns. So instead of saying *Massachusetts voters chose Kennedy because the voters saw Kennedy as a concerned native son,* we can say *Massachusetts voters chose Kennedy because they saw him as a concerned native son.*

Secondly, the many forms of the pronoun are a result of the fact that a pronoun must agree with the noun whose place it is taking. If the noun is plural, the pronoun must be plural; if the noun is feminine, the pronoun must be feminine.

ADJECTIVE: This is easy: it is a word that describes or limits a noun, like *small horse, big dinner, red coat, ten cents, this book, a wall.* Adjectives have one special property; they can indicate the three degrees of a quality named: the positive (*She is a neat dresser.*), the comparative (*She is a neater dresser than her sister.*), and the superlative degree (*She is the neatest dresser in her class.*).

VERB: A verb is the most important word in the sentence. It is the single necessary word. *Stop!* is a grammatical sentence. Every grammatical sentence must contain at least one verb, and it must be a particular kind of verb form. This is what you must understand.

While it is quite true that a verb expresses action or state of being (the usual definitions), it is even more important to remember that a verb is the word we use to show changes in the *time* of an action. The difference in verb forms between *She eats dinner* and *She ate dinner* is slight, but the difference in time is the difference between a present action and a past action. Tense is the term we use for the time of an action. Here is the crux of the verb's role: *every grammatical sentence has to contain a verb that indicates tense.*

It would be helpful if all verb forms showed tense, but unfortunately they do not. In fact, only two of a verb's five principal parts can, alone, indicate tense. These are the present form (*eats*) and the past form (*ate*). Two of the other parts are called participles: a present participle (*eating*) and a past participle (*eaten*). Participles alone do not indicate tense. You do not say *She eating dinner* or *She eaten dinner*. And the fifth principal part (*to eat*), called an infinitive, similarly does not show tense. *She to eat dinner* is not grammatical.

Participles and infinitives are known as VERBALS: they look like verbs but alone they cannot show tense. Consequently, verbals alone cannot be used as the main verb of a sentence. Verbals, however, when used together with helping verbs like *is, were, must, should,* etc., can be used as main verbs. This union of verbal and a helping verb gives us a wide range in describing an action and its timing:

She is eating.

She had been eating.

She should have been eating.

She had eaten.

She may have eaten.

She may have been eating.

Tense is not the whole story of verbs. Eventually, you should spend some time with the full-scale discussion of principal parts in a conventional grammar. There are many strict and complex rules. But if you can grasp at this point the significance of tense and the possibility of defining your meanings with verbs and verb phrases, you are off to a good start.

ADVERB: Someone has said that if you are not sure which part of speech to call a word, call it an adverb. Chances are it will be. At least, grammarians over the years have called some strange words adverbs. For our purposes, you need only remember that adverbs are words that modify verbs and whole sentences. Adverbs modify verbs in three ways: they tell when an action occurs (*now, today*), where it occurs (*below, outside*), or how it occurs (*quickly, slowly*). An adverb can also modify a complete sentence (*Finally, the play began*).

PREPOSITION: To connect sentence elements is an important grammatical function. Prepositions are the words used to relate one noun to another noun or to a verb. For example, consider the phrase *the rowboat near the buoy*: the preposition *near* shows the relationship between *rowboat* and *buoy*. Such a relationship may be one of time (*before, after*), space (*in, behind, near*) or a more general kind (*of, with*).

A preposition always has an object. The noun that follows a preposition is called its object.

CONJUNCTION: Conjunctions connect pairs or series of similar words or groups of words and show the relationship between them. *And* is probably the most commonly used conjunction: *bright and clean, gun and holster*. There are three types:

- Subordinating conjunctions are words like *although, unless, before, if*. Their only purpose is to introduce dependent clauses and at the same time connect them to independent clauses.

Although I am tired, I will go.

You may leave when your relief arrives.

I will take it because I have to leave.

- Coordinating conjunctions (*and, but, for, or, so, nor, yet*) and correlative conjunctions (*either . . . or, neither . . . nor, not only . . . but also*) join equal grammatical units—two nouns, two adjectives, two independent clauses.

The soldiers tried but failed.

The coach yelled a warning, but the guard missed the block.

Either he shows up on time or he is fired.

Unemployment increased not only in the West but also in the South.

INTERJECTION: An interjection expresses emotion or surprise (*Great! Crazy!*). It is not grammatically related to other words in the sentence. Normally, an interjection is followed by a comma. If the interjection is strong, an exclamation point is used.

Word Use

With these parts of speech to build on, we can look now at some of the special ways words are used in sentences. A noun, for example, may be a subject, an object, an indirect object, an object of a preposition, or an objective complement. The exact function is determined by the word's use in a sentence.

SUBJECT: A subject is a noun, pronoun, or noun phrase that names or indicates what the sentence is about. Usually, but not always, the subject appears at the beginning of a sentence.

The police car careened around the corner.
(Subject *car* comes near beginning.)

Around the corner careened the police car.
(Subject *car* comes last.)

DIRECT OBJECT: A direct object is a noun or pronoun that receives the action of a verb. It often answers the question *what?* or *whom?* Normally, it comes right after the verb.

The committee elected its chairperson.

The dogs chased the deer across the field.

Did you see Ann and him at the concert?

INDIRECT OBJECT: A sentence which includes a direct object may also have another complement. When such a word appears between the verb and the direct object, it is called an indirect object. It tells without use of a preposition *to whom* or *to what* something was done. Pronouns used as indirect objects are always in the objective case.

I gave the <u>client</u> my report.

I offered <u>him</u> a bonus.

Note the difference, however, between these sentences: *She called me a waiter* and *She called me a bore*. Here are diagrams of the two:

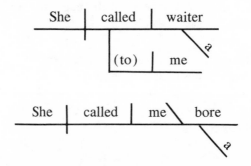

In the first sentence, the indirect object *me* and the direct object *waiter* refer to different persons. In the second, *me* and *bore* refer to the same person. The rule here is that if a sentence has two complements which refer to the same person or thing, the first is the direct object and the second is called an objective complement.

OBJECT OF PREPOSITION: The object of a preposition is the noun or pronoun that completes the relationship defined by the preposition. The preposition, object, and all its modifiers make up a prepositional phrase, which can be used as adjective, adverb, or noun.

In the alley he saw a shadow.

Between him and me there is no argument.

He gave the passes to Cheevers and me.

APPOSITIVE: An appositive is a word or a group of words that comes after a noun or pronoun and expresses its meaning in different words. It is always set off by commas.

My friend, the lawyer, has arrived.

We visited Richmond, the capital of Virginia.

PREDICATE NOUN: A predicate noun (or pronoun) is one type of subject complement in a linking sentence. It comes after the verb, answers the question who or what, and represents the same person or thing as the subject. If it is a pronoun, it is always in the nominative case.

The foreman is Jasper Lewis.

They are the men in blue.

The men in blue are they.

PREDICATE ADJECTIVE: As another type of subject complement, a predicate adjective modifies a subject but comes after the linking verb.

The carnation smells <u>sweet</u>.

The musical score was <u>difficult</u> to follow.

Phrases

In this and the next section we will pass to the groups of words made up of combinations of parts of speech: first phrases, then clauses.

A phrase is a group of related words without a subject and a finite (tense expressing) verb (*in the sunlight, writing the letter, to get the cash*). According to their distinguishing words, the most common phrases are listed below.

NOUN PHRASE: This is a group of nouns having a single meaning and used as a single noun.

He belongs to the <u>Cleveland</u> <u>Browns</u>.

He joined the <u>American</u> <u>Legion</u>.

VERB PHRASE: A verb phrase includes the main verb, any helping verbs, and modifiers.

I <u>will</u> <u>be</u> <u>flying</u> <u>tomorrow</u>.

119

PREPOSITIONAL PHRASE: This is a preposition with its object and modifiers. Normally it functions as an adjective or adverb, sometimes as a noun.

The policeman <u>with</u> <u>the</u> <u>motor</u> <u>bike</u> is the one. (as adjective)

The prisoner climbed <u>over</u> <u>the</u> <u>wall</u>. (as adverb)

<u>After</u> <u>dinner</u> is the best part of the day. (as noun)

PARTICIPIAL PHRASE: Like single participles, these phrases are used as adjectives. Such phrases consist of a participle and any objects or modifiers. Participial phrases may contain either a present or past participle.

<u>Kicking</u> <u>the</u> <u>soccer</u> <u>ball</u>, he turned to the left.

The book <u>lost</u> <u>in</u> <u>the</u> <u>pile</u> was mine.

GERUND PHRASE: This includes a gerund with any modifiers and object. It is used as a noun.

<u>Chopping</u> <u>wood</u> is hard work.

INFINITIVE PHRASE: An infinitive phrase includes an infinitive with its modifiers, subject, or object. It can be used as an adjective, adverb, or noun.

The person to see is the secretary. (adjective)

He is quitting to find a better job. (adverb)

He wanted to run home. (noun)

ABSOLUTE PHRASE: This consists of a noun or pronoun and a participle which modify a whole sentence or clause. It is grammatically unrelated to the rest of the sentence.

The play having ended, we left the theater.

Clauses

A clause is a group of words that contains a subject and verb and forms part or all of a sentence. The chief difference between a clause and a phrase is that the clause has a subject and verb and the phrase does not. There are two kinds of clauses—independent and dependent.

An independent clause is the principal part of the sentence, the part that makes the most important statement. Without it, a sentence would be incomplete. An independent clause can stand by itself in a simple sentence, expressing a complete thought. An independent clause is also a necessary part of a compound, complex, and compound-complex sentence. In the following examples the independent clause is underlined; the dependent is not.

He is a team player who never quits.

When he finished the tax form, he began to groan.

The books which he borrowed are overdue.

Note that each of the independent clauses could stand as a complete sentence: *He is a team player. He began to groan. The books are overdue.*

Dependent clauses cannot stand alone. They are always joined to an independent clause or they are sentence fragments. Dependent clauses are usually introduced by relative pronouns or subordinating conjunctions like *who, when, which, that, because, as,* and *since.* Dependent clauses are used as nouns, adjectives, and adverbs.

NOUN CLAUSES: A noun clause may be used in any way that an individual noun can be used: as subject, object, object of preposition, predicate noun, etc. Noun clauses are usually introduced by *that, what, how, however, why, whether,* and *whoever.*

That he was guilty was plain to all. (subject)

He believes whatever he hears. (object)

I couldn't see the accident from where we stood. (object of preposition)

My guess is that it will rain. (predicate noun)

ADJECTIVE CLAUSES: An adjective clause is used as a single adjective to modify a noun or pronoun. Most adjective clauses are introduced by a relative pronoun like *who, which,* or *that.*

I lost the watch which my father gave me.

The house where Mark Twain lived in his final years is in Hartford.

ADVERB CLAUSES: An adverb clause does the work of an adverb, telling when, where, why, or under what condition an action takes place.

When it snows, I leave for Florida.

We drive wherever the roads lead.

Because he forgot his keys, he could not get in.

If the job is offered, I will accept.

Sentences

Sentences are divided into three basic types, according to their construction: simple, compound, and complex. There are also various combinations of the compound and complex. Essentially, these divisions are based on the number and kind of clauses in the particular sentence.

SIMPLE SENTENCES: A simple sentence contains only one group of words having a subject and verb and expressing a complete thought. The subject and verb may each be single or either or both may be compound. In a simple sentence the nouns form one related group and the verbs form one related group. In compound and complex sentences, which contain more than one clause, there is a separate subject group and a separate verb group in each clause.

Charlotte worked at home. (single subject, single verb)

The speaker roared and ranted. (single subject, compound verb)

The lawyer and his associate appeared in court. (compound subject, single verb)

The soldiers and the marines fought and died. (compound subject, compound verb)

125

COMPOUND SENTENCES: A compound sentence contains two or more independent clauses (simple sentences). The clauses must be closely related in sense and separated by one of the coordinating conjunctions or by punctuation.

The president said there would be action, but he did not promise an attack.

The whistle blew; the workers ran toward the gate.

A compound sentence may also contain one or more dependent clauses along with its two independent clauses. (This construction is often called a compound-complex sentence.)

The new employee registered when he arrived, and then he went to the infirmary where he had to wait in a long line.

COMPLEX SENTENCES: A complex sentence contains one independent clause and one or more dependent clauses.

Jay Parsons, who works in this building, is a CPA.

The town went wild when the hostages were freed.

Common Grammatical Errors

SENTENCE FRAGMENTS: A sentence fragment occurs when a writer punctuates part of a sentence as if it were a complete sentence. A sentence contains a subject, a verb, and a complete idea. A sentence fragment lacks one of these three elements. It is a serious error because it means that the writer cannot recognize a complete sentence. Two common types of fragments are dependent clauses and verbal phrases that are punctuated as complete sentences.

SENTENCE FRAGMENTS: *Because he could find no work.*

Having been angered by him once.

CORRECTIONS: *Because he could find no work, he left the area.* (Dependent clause now attached to an independent clause.)

He had been angered by him once before. (Verbal changed into verb.)

RUN-ON SENTENCES: This error happens when two independent clauses are run together without any punctuation. The two independent clauses should be joined by a coordinating conjunction or separated by appropriate punctuation. The error is a bad one, because it indicates that the writer cannot identify the basic unit of all writing—the sentence.

RUN-ON SENTENCE: *I have been here three days my partner just arrived.*

CORRECTIONS: *I have been here three days; my partner just arrived.*

I have been here three days, but my partner just arrived.

COMMA SPLICES: A comma splice occurs when two independent clauses are joined with only a comma. The error reflects a failure in grammar rather than punctuation. It suggests that the writer still cannot recognize a sentence.

COMMA SPLICE: *The jury stayed out five hours, he was plainly guilty.*

CORRECTIONS: *The jury stayed out five hours, but he was plainly guilty.*

The jury stayed out five hours; he was plainly guilty.

The jury stayed out five hours; however,* he was plainly guilty.

Although the jury stayed out five hours, he was plainly guilty.

IRREGULAR VERBS: There are several irregular verb forms that trouble some writers. The best advice is to memorize their principal parts: present, past, past participle, and present participle.

- sit (to be seated):   sit, sat, sat, sitting

- set (to put or place):   set, set, set, setting

- rise (to stand):   rise, rose, risen, rising

- raise (to elevate):   raise, raised, raised, raising

- lie (to recline):   lie, lay, lain, lying

- lay (to cause to lie):   lay, laid, laid, laying

AGREEMENT OF SUBJECT AND VERB: A verb must agree with its subject in number: single subjects require singular verbs; plural subjects need plural verbs. There are few agreement problems when the verb immediately follows the subject in a normal subject-verb-object order. The problem

---

*Words like *however, nevertheless, moreover* are called conjunctive adverbs. They are always preceded by a semicolon when they join independent clauses.

begins when words intervene between the real subject and the real verb. Remember these guidelines:

- Identify the subject and verb in every clause. Do not be fooled by anything that separates them.

> *One of the workers was chosen to be foreman.*

> *The sales manager, along with his salesmen, deserves praise.*

> *The bridge between the cliffs is very old.*

> *He, together with Bob and Harry, was late.*

Compound subjects connected by *and, both . . . and,* and similar conjunctions require plural verbs.

> *He and Bob were competing for the promotion.*

> *Both the pilot and the copilot were on standby.*

Compound subjects connected by *or, either . . . or, neither . . . nor* require singular verbs if the parts are singular, plural verbs if they are plural.

> *Neither the secretary nor her assistant is present.*

> *Neither the clerks nor the typists were satisfied.*

In sentences beginning with *there* or *here,* the verb is singular or plural depending on whether the real subject, which comes after the verb, is singular or plural.

There is a car in the garage.

Here are the rules of the game.

- A collective noun (*team, class,* and the like) is singular when the group is acting as a unit, plural when the members of the group are acting as individuals.

The board has agreed on a course of action.

The board were divided on a course of action.

- Indefinite pronouns (*everybody, every one, somebody, someone, anybody, any one*) and words modified by *every* or *each* are always singular and when used as a subject require a singular verb.

Everybody in both offices was ready.

Every one of the illustrations was flawed.

- When the subject is plural in form but singular in meaning, the rule changes:

  (1) Nouns expressing quantities, distance, and sums can be either singular or plural.

Five pounds of salt is (are) allowed each patron.

A million dollars was (were) spent.

Ten miles of road is (are) needed.

(2) Use a singular verb with titles.

The Principles of Economics *is our text*.

(3) Use a singular verb with plural words used as words, not as the names of the objects.

"Auditors" is a common noun.

(4) Nouns that are plural in form but singular in meaning (*news, politics, civics, measles,* etc.) require a singular verb.

The news gets better and better.

Politics is a dirty business.

On the other hand, certain words of this type (*riches, scissors, trousers, goods, athletics*) require a plural verb.

The scissors are on the counter.

His trousers were unpressed.

Athletics are critical to this program.

DANGLING MODIFIERS: A modifier "dangles" when it is not clearly related to some word in the sentence. Verbal phrases are especially liable to this often silly error.

DANGLING MODIFIER: *Hanging his new title over the door, the ladder slipped and John fell.*

CORRECTIONS: *Hanging his new title over the door, John fell when the ladder slipped.*

When John was hanging his new title over the door, the ladder slipped and he fell.

PRONOUNS AND ANTECEDENTS: The relative pronoun (*who, which, that*) that introduces a dependent clause must have a clear-cut word to which it refers (its antecedent) in the independent clause. It is this antecedent that determines the person and number of the verb in the dependent clause. Careless handling of the pronoun and antecedent can cause errors in reference and agreement.

REFERENCE FAULT: *The windows were smashed by the high winds which made him nervous.*

CORRECTION: *The windows were smashed by the high winds, a mishap which made him nervous.*

AGREEMENT FAULT: *The first of the Super Bowl players who was introduced was the left end.*

CORRECTION: *The first of the Super Bowl players who were introduced was the left end.*

WHO OR WHOM: How do you choose between these pronouns? The choice depends on the function of the word within its clause. If the pronoun is the subject of the verb, use *who*; if it is the object of the verb or preposition, use *whom*. One quick way to decide is to see if there is any word before the verb that could be a subject. If there is not (*who ran, who were late*), the relative pronoun must be the subject, and *who* is correct. If the verb already has a subject (*whom I love, whom the cat scratched*), the relative pronoun must be its object, and *whom* is the right choice.

Punctuation

Most readers agree that periods, commas, and capitals in the right places make for easier reading. The problem for writers is to find those "right places." We have been hearing the directions most of our school lives, but unfortunately they are not easy to follow. Too often they include some mention of "absolute phrases," "nonrestrictive words," and "appositional clauses"—meaningless terms to many of us.

Some writing teachers have skirted the jargon by relating punctuation to the tones and gestures we use in speaking. You can decide on punctuation, these teachers claim, by imagining what pauses and pitch you would use if you were speaking. A short pause calls for a comma, a longer one for a period. When someone finishes a statement, he lowers the pitch of his voice. After a question, he usually raises the pitch. If you can "hear" punctuation, by all means try this approach. Coupled with a reminder that all punctuation is designed to help a reader grasp meaning, this approach will give you a clue to the major punctuation marks.

You will have even more confidence about punctuation when you have mastered a few principles. Most of these are based on an understanding of the simple sentence. If you cannot recognize a complete sentence, there is no way you will be able to punctuate it correctly. Once you have mastered that, other rules of punctuation will begin to fall into place. And be encouraged by the fact that there are very few rules of punctuation. Here—in about a page—are all the important ones:

PERIOD: (1) at the end of declarative (statement) and imperative (command) sentences

                 (2) after abbreviations

COLON: (1) to introduce long quotations

                 (2) to set off a series

SEMICOLON: (1) to separate independent clauses in a compound sentence that does not contain a coordinating conjunction

                 (2) to separate items of a series already punctuated by commas

COMMA: (1) to separate independent clauses joined by a coordinating conjunction

                 (2) to separate items in a series

                 (3) to set off nonrestrictive material

                 (4) to set off appositives and parenthetical expressions

                 (5) after an introductory (especially long) adverbial phrase or participle phrase

(6) to set off elements that are grammatically independent (direct address, absolute constructions, etc.)

(7) to set off elements in dates, addresses,
and place names

The functions of the other punctuation marks—dash, question mark, exclamation, quotation mark, parenthesis—are
obvious or readily grasped after a quick review.

Basically, in all our writing we use punctuation

- to separate,

- to introduce, and

- to enclose.

For example, we use a period to separate one sentence from
another, a colon to introduce a series, and a pair of commas
to enclose parenthetical expressions within sentences. Below
you will see how many punctuation problems can be con-
tained and clarified within these three concepts of separation,
introduction, and enclosure. We will only be concerned with
the most commonly used—and most troublesome—punctuation. You can find additional information in dictionaries and
composition books.

Punctuation to SEPARATE

- Words, phrases, short clauses in a series—**COMMA**

  I packed my shirts, pants, and underwear.

  He ran, he passed, and he kicked with great skill.

- Declarative and imperative sentences from other sentences —**PERIOD**

  The plan failed in every detail.

  Leave at once.

- Independent clauses of a compound sentence joined by a coordinating conjunction—**COMMA**

  There was little to be said, for he was plainly guilty.

  Those on the outside were saved, but those within perished.

- Independent clauses of a compound sentence joined without a coordinating conjunction—**SEMICOLON**

The advance party has been here for weeks; the main body has just arrived.

Computer courses are required of all business majors; consequently, the classes are large.

- Introductory adverbial clauses and participle phrases— **COMMA**

Because he had left his samples home, he was not able to demonstrate.

Having read the report, I was prepared for the interview.

Punctuation to INTRODUCE

- Series—**COLON**
  A colon is used to introduce several different elements as the following examples show.

  After the salutation in a business letter:
  Gentlemen:
  Ladies:

  Before a series of appositives:
  I enjoyed three parts of the play: the opening scene, the second act, and the final scene.

To introduce a list:
> *The customer ordered the following: a sandwich, dessert, and coffee.*

Between two clauses when the second explains the first:
> *He is certain of his future: he will become a consultant.*

To separate numerals (12:10 p.m.), biblical references (23:10), and titles from subtitles (*Natural Landscaping: An Energy-Saving Alternative*)

- Abrupt break in thought or hesitation—**DASH**

> *I—but I don't want to go.*

> *I want to—no, I'd better stay home and work.*

- An emphatic appositive—**DASH**

> *He had only one interest—gambling.*

> *The stock market—a bullish market—declined for a second day.*

- Conversation or short quotation—**COMMA**

> *The coach was so pleased and excited by his team's performance that he shouted, "That's the way to go!"*

> *Who said, "Patriotism is the last refuge of scoundrels"?*

- Long quotation—**COLON**

> A colon introduces a quotation of more than five lines.

Punctuation to ENCLOSE

- Nonrestrictive clauses and phrases (those not essential to the meaning of a sentence)—**COMMAS**

  My resignation, which I offered to my supervisor, was accepted.

  The Wall Street Journal, *my favorite newspaper, has an outstanding front page.*

- Parenthetical elements (words and phrases that interrupt a sentence but do not modify a particular part) and nouns of address—**COMMAS**

  This is, just between you and me, not the way to go.

  He is, I believe, ill-advised.

  All those in favor, raise your hands.

  Call me when you arrive, will you, John?

- Appositives (words or phrases that explain the word they immediately follow)—**COMMAS**

  His uncle, a long-time fisherman, was up early and on his way to the river.

  I told my son, a boy of eight, to go to bed.

● Addresses and dates—**COMMAS**

.

I joined the Navy on March 27, 1978, in New Haven, Connecticut.

Since August, 1968, my home has been Adler Plains, New Jersey.

He has lived in St. Louis, Missouri, most of his life.

He came to work on 12 June 1979. (No comma when the day precedes the month.)

● Conversation and direct quotations—**COMMAS and QUOTATION MARKS**

(1) *"I've had enough," he said.*

"What brought this on?" I asked.

"Because," he replied, "for the last week I have been taking nothing but abuse from Marty."

"That's hard to believe," I said. "Have you talked to your supervisor?"

(2) *My friend said, "My favorite musical is 'West Side Story.'"*

(3) *"I hope that's the end of it," the foreman said; "I've been too patient."*

● Titles of short stories, poems, paintings, songs, essays, chapters of books—**QUOTATION MARKS**

"The Bear" is one of Faulkner's best short stories.

"The Star Spangled Banner" is really difficult to sing.

- Titles of books—**UNDERLINE or ITALICS**

All Quiet on the Western Front is a devastating account of trench warfare.

Spelling

Poor spelling is a mortal sin in written English. For many readers, misspellings are indisputable evidence of incompetence—at least, of carelessness.

Anyone can improve his spelling. It is a matter of self-discipline. Try some of these suggestions:

- Pronounce words carefully (*ath-let-ic, ac-com-mo-date, en-vi-ron-ment*).

- Look closely at difficult words. Visualize the correct spelling. Try to see the word on a mental page.

- When in doubt about a word's spelling, check it out in a dictionary.

- Keep your own list of recurrent spelling errors. Devise some scheme to remember the correct spelling (2 c's and 2 m's in *accommodate*, 2 a's in *separate*, station*ery* is used to write a lett*er*).

- Learn and use spelling rules.

- Proofread, proofread, proofread—as many times as possible.

144

Spelling Rules

Most spelling rules are not foolproof. Some rules have so many qualifications and exceptions that they are all but useless. The rules that follow are the best we have. They can be trusted in nearly all cases.

Before you can use these rules, you must be able to distinguish between a prefix and a suffix. A prefix is something put before a word to change its meaning. A suffix is put at the end of a word to change its meaning.

- **PREFIX**

  dis (prefix) + *satisfy* (root) = *dissatisfy*

  un (prefix) + *usual* (root) = *unusual*

- **SUFFIX**

  final (root) + *ly* (suffix) = *finally*

  nine (root) + *ty* (suffix) = *ninety*

Now for the rules:

- Double a final consonant before a suffix when the consonant ends a one-syllable word and is preceded by a single vowel.

plan	*planned*
drop	*dropping*
stop	*stopped*

- Double a final consonant before a suffix when the consonant ends an accented syllable of the word and is preceded by a single vowel.

control	*controller*
occur	*occurring*
confer	*conferring*

- A word ending in silent *e* usually drops the *e* before a suffix beginning with a vowel, but retains the *e* before a suffix beginning with a consonant.

arrange	*arranging*	*arrangement*
care	*caring*	*careful*
like	*likable*	*likeness*

- Most plurals are formed by adding *s* or *es* to the singular. But there are many exceptions. Check your dictionary for plural spellings. To make the plural of a noun ending in *y* preceded by a consonant, change the *y* to *i* and add *es*. If a vowel precedes the *y*, add the *s* directly.

girl	*girls*
bush	*bushes*
sky	*skies*
fly	*flies*
valley	*valleys*
monkey	*monkeys*

Spelling List

These words are frequently misspelled. Learn to spell the first five words on the list. Once you have mastered these, move on to the next five. The time you spend here will be clearly reflected in improved spelling.

1. absence
   accidentally
   accommodate
   accumulate
   acquainted

2. across
   all right
   already
   athlete
   attendance

3. beginning
   believe
   benefited
   brilliant
   business

4. calendar
   capital (city)
   capitol (building)
   cavalry
   cemetery

5. changeable
   coarse
   committee
   comparative
   conscientious

6. convenience
   definite
   desert
   desirable
   dessert

7. dining
   disappear
   disappoint
   disease
   decrease

8. eighth
   embarrass
   environment
   equipped
   especially

9. exaggerate
   existence
   extracurricular
   extravagant
   extremely

10. familiar
    fascination
    February
    fictitious
    foreign

11. government
    grammar
    guarantee
    guidance
    height

12. hindrance
    huge
    hurriedly
    hypocrisy
    immediately

13. inadequate
    incidentally
    independent
    initiation
    intelligence

14. irresistible
    knowledge
    laboratory
    leisurely
    librarian

15. lightning
    loneliness
    maintenance
    maneuver
    medieval

16. miniature
    misspelled
    necessary
    nickel
    niece

17. noticeable
    obedience
    occasion
    occurred
    official

18. omitted
    pamphlet
    parallel
    pastime
    perform

19. permissible
    perseverance
    persistent
    personnel
    pneumonia

20. possession
    preceding
    preference
    prevalent
    primitive

21. privilege
    professor
    psychology
    quiet
    quite

22. recommend
    religious
    repetitious
    resistance
    restaurant

23. ridiculous
    schedule
    seize
    sense
    separate

24. sergeant
    severely
    similar
    sophomore
    sponsor

25. stationary (fixed)
    stationery (paper)
    studying
    successful
    superintendent

26. supersede
    surprise
    synonym
    thorough
    tendency

27. tragedy
    truly
    tyranny
    twelfth
    undoubtedly

28. unnecessary
    until
    usually
    vegetables
    vengeance

29. vertical
    villain
    warrant
    weather
    weird

30. whether
    who's (who is)
    whose
    won't
    writing